THEMATIC UNIT
Bears

Written by Sarah Kartcher Clark, M.A.

Teacher Created Resources, Inc.
6421 Industry Way
Westminster, CA 92683
www.teachercreated.com
©*2002 Teacher Created Resources, Inc.*
Reprinted, 2005
Made in U.S.A.
ISBN-0-7439-3062-2

Illustrated by
Victoria Ponikvar-Frasier
Edited by
Melissa Hart, M.F.A.
Contributing Editor
Mara Ellen Guckian
Cover Art by
Brenda DiAntonis

Table of Contents

Introduction

Bears contains a comprehensive, whole language, thematic unit about many types of bears, real and fictional. Its 80 exciting pages are filled with a variety of lesson ideas and reproducible pages designed for preschool-aged children. At its core are three high-quality children's literature selections: *My Friend Bear, Bears are Curious,* and *Touch the Sky, My Little Bear.*

There are activities for each literature selection which set the stage for reading, encourage enjoyment of the books, and elaborate on themes. Activities that integrate language arts, math, science, social studies, art, music, and life skills are also provided. Unit management tools include time-saving devices such as patterns for bulletin boards and learning centers.

This thematic unit includes:

- ❏ **literature selections**—summaries of three children's books with related lessons (complete with reproducible pages) across the curriculum

- ❏ **poetry**—suggested selections and lessons enabling students to write and publish their own work

- ❏ **planning guides**—suggestions for sequencing lessons during each day of the unit, and ideas for making projects

- ❏ **bulletin board ideas**—suggestions and plans for student-created and/or interactive bulletin boards

- ❏ **unit management suggestions**—teacher aids for organizing the unit, plus incentives and patterns

- ❏ **curriculum connections**—projects which integrate language, math, science, social studies, art, music, physical education, and life skills

- ❏ **culminating activities**—these require students to synthesize their learning to create a product or engage in an activity that can be shared with others

- ❏ **bibliography**—suggestions for additional literature and nonfiction books on the theme

> **To keep this valuable resource intact so it can be used year after year, you may wish to punch holes in the pages and store them in a three-ring binder.**

Introduction *(cont.)*

Why a Balanced Approach?

The strength of a balanced language approach is that it involves children in using all modes of communication—reading, writing, listening, illustrating, and speaking. Communication skills are interconnected and integrated into lessons that emphasize the whole of language. Implicit in this approach is our knowledge that every whole—including individual words—is composed of parts, and that directed study of those parts can help a child to master the whole. Experience and research tell us that regular attention to phonics and other word–attack skills develops reading mastery, thereby addressing the unity of the whole language experience. The child is thus led to read, write, spell, speak, and listen confidently in response to a literature experience introduced by the teacher. In these ways, language skills grow rapidly, stimulated by direct practice, involvement, and interest in the topic at hand.

Why Thematic Planning?

One very useful tool for implementing an integrated whole language program is thematic planning. By choosing a theme with correlating literature selections for a unit of study, a teacher can plan activities throughout the day that lead to a cohesive, in-depth study of the topic. Children then practice and apply their skills in meaningful contexts. Consequently, they learn and retain more. Both teachers and students are freed from a day that is broken into unrelated segments of isolated drill and practice.

Why Cooperative Learning?

Along with academic skills and content, students need to learn social skills. This area of development can no longer be taken for granted. Students must learn to work cooperatively in groups in order to function well in modern society. Group activities should be a regular part of school life, and teachers should consciously include social objectives as well as academic objectives in their planning. Younger children, in whom cooperative learning skills are not yet fully developed, can work together to follow a recipe, sing songs, share materials and equipment, and discuss ideas and thoughts as a group while reading books aloud. Teachers can model cooperative behaviors such as politely listening to other students and raising a hand to indicate the desire to speak. Opportunities to reinforce cooperative learning in young children can be found on a daily basis.

Why Big Books?

An excellent cooperative, whole language activity is the production of Big Books. Groups of students, or the whole class, can apply their language skills, content knowledge, and creativity to produce a Big Book that may become a part of the classroom library for reading and rereading. These books make excellent culminating projects to share beyond the classroom with parents, librarians, and other classes.

My Friend Bear

by Jez Alborough

Summary

This is the warm and fuzzy fictional story of a boy who becomes friends with a bear. Eddie has a stuffed teddy bear named Freddie. Eddie loves Freddie and considers him a friend, but he is sad because his teddy bear friend cannot talk. As Eddie and Freddie are walking through a forest, they happen upon a huge stuffed teddy bear. They are amazed. Eddie wonders to whom the teddy bear belongs. Suddenly they hear some snuffling and scuffling, and so Eddie and his teddy quickly hide behind the big stuffed bear.

Eddie soon learns to whom the teddy bear belongs. The big bear and Eddie become new friends and learn the joy of having both a real and an imaginary friend.

Sample Plan

Day 1

- Ask students to think of a teddy bear. Do they have a teddy bear they call a friend?

- Read *My Friend Bear* to the whole class.

- Discuss friendship as a class.

- Have students introduce their teddy bears.

- Have students work on a friendship quilt (page 8).

Day 2

- Practice number recognition by matching the bears (page 39).

- Have students write a letter to their teddy bear (page 33).

- Select some bear songs and finger plays to do as a class (page 58).

- Help Eddie find his teddy, Freddie (page 9).

- Select bear art activities to complete (pages 53–56).

Day 3

- Discuss rhyming words. Read *My Friend Bear* to the whole class again. Have students look for words that rhyme (page 35).

- Determine the size of a bear. Complete the "How Big is a Bear?" activity (page 45).

Day 4

- Sit in a large circle with teddy bears. Organize and carry out the "Classifying and Sorting" activity (page 46).

- Have students practice counting skills with "Bear Counters" (page 37).

- Select bear art activities to complete (pages 53–56).

- Make a "Quiet Time Teddy" for each student to dress (pages 59–60).

Day 5

- Read other stories about teddy bears (see local library and bibliography on page 79 for suggestions).

- Put together "My Teddy and Me" books with students (page 11).

- Select "Bear-y Fun Games" to play with students (page 57).

- Organize and carry out the Teddy Bear Picnic (page 67).

Overview of Activities

Setting the Stage

1. Assemble the "Beary Good Work" bulletin board following the directions on page 75. Set up the activities, awards, door handles, and other materials described in the Unit Management section beginning on page 70. Send home the letter to parents announcing the start of the unit and requesting materials and permission for students to bring teddy bears to school. Along with the parent letter, send home a copy of the skills and objectives on page 70 to keep parents informed as to what is being taught in school.

2. Introduce the unit on bears to the students by displaying the class teddy bear (see pattern on pages 76–78). Explain to students that they will get a chance to share their teddy bear with the class. (Remember to bring extra teddy bears to school for those students who may not have one.)

3. Discuss friendship with the class. What are friends? What can you do with friends? Can a teddy bear be a friend? How is a teddy bear a friend?

4. Ask students the following questions prior to reading the story:

   How many of you have a teddy bear?

   What are some of the memorable moments you've had with your teddy bear?

   What is the name of your teddy bear?

   How has your teddy bear been a good friend to you?

   Is your teddy bear big or small? Describe your teddy bear.

5. Gather students together in a circle and show them the cover of the book, *My Friend Bear*. Have students share predictions of what they think the book will be about. Talk about the cover. Ask students to be listening for the word *friend*.

Enjoying the Book

1. Read the book aloud to students. They will enjoy this story. Be sure to spend plenty of time looking at the pictures, and allow time for students to ask questions. After the book has been read, ask students to share what they liked about the book. What did they learn about friends from this book? Do they have a teddy bear friend who resembles the great big silly bear or the little boy's teddy, Freddie?

2. Discuss the order of the events in the story. Let the children know that sequence is another word for order. Have students work together to retell the story, recalling the events in order. Ask simple questions to check their comprehension of the story.

3. Once all students have brought their teddy bears to school, make time for each student to introduce and share his/her teddy bear with the class. Allow students to ask questions about each teddy bear.

Overview of Activities *(cont.)*

4. Give directions and begin working on the friendship quilt (page 8). You may choose to do this activity over the course of one or more days. Hang the friendship quilt in your classroom when it is completed.

5. Have students tell a story about two bears who are friends. Students can work in groups of two or three. Let them come up with their own story. (The stories will probably be short.) Students might also use puppets to retell the story. You may choose to make the bear puppets or the bear masks to be used for these student-created stories. (See pages 53–55 for instructions and patterns for the bear mask and bear puppet.)

6. Have available a basket of books about bears and teddy bears. Read a few books from the basket and compare the stories about teddy bears. How are they alike? How are they different? (See the bibliography on page 79 for a detailed list of books about bears for young children.)

Extending the Book

1. After finishing the story *My Friend Bear*, have students "write" a sequel to the story about Eddie, Freddie, and the great big silly bear. Each student will be responsible for a different page in the story. You can write the words for the students, then have them illustrate their page. Compile these pages into a Big Book that can be placed in the class library. The title of this book could be *The Teddy Bear Sequel*, or you may choose to come up with another title as a class.

2. Design and incorporate classroom activities based on bears and teddy bears. Math, reading, science, art, and life skills lessons and activities correlate with *My Friend Bear*.

3. Select possibly unfamiliar words from the story. Write these words and teach students their meanings. Use the words in a sentence. Point them out when they are used in conversation or in other books.

4. If possible, search for information about Jez Alborough, the author of this book. Candlewick Press has a website with information on this author. Discuss with students what the author and illustrator do when making a book. If possible, read other books by this same author or illustrator. Some examples of other books are: *It's the Bear!* (Candlewick Press, 1994), *Where's My Teddy?* (Candlewick Press, 1992), and *Hug!* (Candlewick Press, 2000).

5. Select art activities that you would like to complete as a class (page 53–56).

Friendship Quilt

Materials:

copy of quilt square for each child

colored paper (optional)

crayons, markers, or colored pencils

yarn

scissors

Directions:

Before you create a friendship quilt, have a class discussion about friendship and the friends that children have in their lives. Why are friends important? What do we like about friends?

Make a copy of the rectangle below on different colors of paper and distribute one to each child. Have students think of a teddy bear or another friend and ask them to draw a picture in the square of something they do with this friend. If possible, have students cut out the square; provide assistance as needed.

To make the friendship quilt, arrange the squares into a quilt design, making a pattern with the colors. Punch two or three holes along each side of the construction paper (***except*** for the squares that will be along the outside edge of the friendship quilt). Tie the squares together, looping yarn through the punched holes. This can teach or reinforce the skill of tying bows. Make a sign that reads "Our Friendship Quilt" and place it at the top of the quilt. Hang the quilt in a prominent place in your classroom.

Where is My Teddy?

Help Eddie find his friend Freddie.

Words that Rhyme

The book *My Friend Bear* has many rhyming words in it. Draw a line connecting the pictures that rhyme.

My Teddy and Me

Directions:

1. Make copies of this page for each student.

2. Working on one teddy bear page at a time, have students dictate words to complete the sentence.

3. Have students draw pictures to illustrate each sentence/page.

4. Once the teddy bear pages have been completed, cut them out. (Some students may need assistance.)

5. Cut out and staple the pages to create a miniature book for students. Be sure to allow time for students to read their books to others.

Bears are Curious

by Joyce Milton

Summary

Bears are Curious *is a nonfiction book designed with the beginning reader in mind. It presents accurate information about three different types of bears—the black bear, the brown bear (otherwise known as the grizzly bear), and the polar bear. It also shows what bears eat and what activities they engage in. The pictures and illustrations give students a good idea of what these bears look like and where they live.*

To illustrate how curious bears are, one of the final pages depicts a bear wandering into somebody's backyard and beginning to eat off the picnic table. The family calls for help. The bear is shot with a tranquilizer and brought back to the forest. Be sure to stress to students that the bear is not hurt! You may choose not to read these last pages if you think that they will disturb your students.

Sample Plan

Day 1

- Brainstorm about bears. What prior knowledge do students have about bears?
- Read *Bears are Curious* to the whole class.
- Discuss the different types of bears discussed in the book.
- Have students act out "Bear Charades" (page 15).
- Begin Daily Language Experience activities and bear journals (pages 30–32).

Day 2

- Practice counting numbers 1–20 with the dot-to-dot (page 38).
- Visit "Virtual Zoos" on the Internet to show students pictures of real bears (page 44).
- Select some "Bear Songs and Finger Plays" to do as a class (page 58).
- Introduce the poetry activities. Share the finished poems as a class (page 35).
- Select bear art activities to complete (pages 53–56).

Day 3

- Figure out what the different types of bears eat (page 47).
- Select "Bear-y Yummy Treats" to make as a class (pages 61–62).

- Learn about bear habitats. Complete the "Bear Habitat" activity (page 45).

Day 4

- Complete the "Bear Facts" activity to learn information about bears (page 16).
- What do bears do all year? Do the "Four Season Fun" activity (page 17).
- Complete the "All About Bears" bear cube (page 19).
- Create the "TV Time!" bear story as a class (page 20).

Day 5

- Read other stories about real bears (see local library and bibliography page 79 for suggestions).
- Review the differences between the bears with the "Which Bear?" activity (page 18).
- Select "Bear-y Fun Games" to play with students (page 57).
- Have students design and create a bear mural (page 68).

Overview of Activities

Setting the Stage

1. Assemble the "Real or Pretend" bulletin board, following the directions on page 75. Set up the activities, awards, door handles, and other materials described in the Unit Management section beginning on page 70.

2. Ask students the following questions prior to reading the story:

   What is a bear?

   What are the different types of bears?

   What does a bear eat?

   Where does a bear live and sleep?

   What else do you know about bears?

3. Using a large piece of butcher paper, write "What do you know about bears?" at the top, and ask students to share with you what they know about bears. (There may be misinformation that is shared. You will need to keep track of it so that you can teach correct information about bears over the course of the unit.)

4. Gather students together in a circle and show them the cover of the book *Bears are Curious*. Talk about the cover. Have students share predictions of what they think the book will be about. Ask students to be listening for the answers to the questions you just asked.

Enjoying the Book

1. Read the book *Bears are Curious* aloud to students. Be sure to spend plenty of time looking at the pictures, and encourage students to ask questions. After the book has been read, ask students to share what they liked about the book. What did they learn about bears from this book? Do they know any more information about bears that was not mentioned in the book?

2. Have available a basket of different books about bears. Read a few books from the basket and compare these stories about bears. How are they alike? How are they different? Is there any more information that you can add to the "What do you know about bears?" chart?

3. Complete the "Bear Facts" activity on page 16. For a review of the information learned from the book, play the "Bear Charades" game on page 15. Lead students in the finger plays and songs found on page 58.

4. Make bear habitats using the information on page 45. Math, reading, science, art, and life skills lessons and activities correlate with *Bears are Curious*.

5. Fill in the classroom newsletter (page 72) and send it home to inform parents about what students are learning in school.

Overview of Activities *(cont.)*

Extending the Book

1. After finishing the story *Bears are Curious*, have students write or tell another story about bears. Compile these stories into a Big Book that can be placed in the class library. The title of this book might be *Our Bear Book*, or you may choose to come up with another title as a class.

2. Select possibly unfamiliar words from the story. Write these words and teach students their meanings. Use them in a sentence. Point out these words when they are used in conversation or in other books.

3. Search for information about the author and illustrator of this book. If possible, read other books by the author, including: *Bats and Other Night Animals* (Random House, 1994); *Gorillas* (Random House, 1997); and *Whales: The Gentle Giants* (Random House, 1989).

4. If possible, watch movies from your school library about bears. Complete the bear paw activity suggested on page 29.

5. Select art activities that you would like to complete as a class (pages 53–56). Don't forget to use the bear awards on page 74 to spread confidence and encouragement in your class.

Bear Charades

After reading the book *Bears are Curious*, students will be able to tell you many things about bears. What are some of the activities that bears engage in? Play a game of bear charades to reinforce information being taught about bears. Cut up the slips of paper below and place them in a bowl. Have your class sit in a circle on the floor. Select one student to take a slip of paper from the bowl. Make sure that the child understands the action on the paper. Then have him/her demonstrate the action and see if the class can guess what it is. Allow any sounds that the student may need to act out the charades. Be sure to give every student a chance to perform a charade. (You can repeat the charades, if necessary.) If students prefer, they can create their own bear actions to act out. Below are suggestions for bear activities:

Bears sniff the air.	**Bears growl.**
Bears take honey from beehives.	**Bears sleep all winter.**
Bears eat flowers.	**Some bears climb trees.**
Bears catch fish.	**Bears can run.**
Polar bears can swim.	**Bears eat beetles and ants.**

The Bear Facts

Materials:

copy of bear face

hangers

index cards

scissors

crayons and markers

yarn

tape

Directions:

1. Color and cut out the bear face.

2. Using tape, attach the bear face to a hanger.

3. On index cards with marker, write down facts about bears that students have learned.

4. Tie the index cards to the hanger with yarn.

5. Hang the bear facts mobile in your classroom to remind students of what they are learning about bears.

Four Season Fun

Draw or paint a picture of what bears do during each of the four seasons.

Spring	Summer

Fall	Winter

Which Bear?

Listen as your teacher reads these sentences. Draw a line from each sentence to the bear it describes.

I am a big white bear.

I am a good tree climber.

I am sometimes called a grizzly bear.

I like to eat honey, ants, flowers, and nuts.

I hunt walrus and seals.

I have very long claws to catch fish.

black bear

brown bear

polar bear

All About Bears

Materials:

- paper plate for each student
- yarn
- crayons
- hole punch

Directions:

1. There are different types of bears. Some of these include black bears, grizzly bears, and polar bears. Have each student select one of these types of bears. Read the book *Bears are Curious* to students and provide other picture books for students to look through in order to research information about the bear they have selected. Spend time interpreting information on the various bears for students. You may even wish to make lists on the chalkboard to show differences between the three types of bears.

2. Once students have the information they need, distribute a paper plate to each student.

3. Have students draw pictures on the paper plate to illustrate the information they have learned about bears. After students have had a turn to share their picture with the rest of the class, hang the paper plates around the classroom.

Polar Bears

- Polar bears live in the Arctic.
- Polar bears have thick fur to keep warm.
- Polar bears hunt seals and walrus.
- Polar bears are good swimmers.

Brown Bears

- Brown bears are also called grizzly bears.
- Brown bears have longer claws than black bears.
- Brown bears can climb trees.
- Brown bears like to catch and eat fish.

Black Bears

- Black bears hibernate all winter.
- Black bears eat ants, beetles, berries, flowers, and honey.
- Black bears are very agile climbers.
- Black bears have an acute sense of smell.

TV Time!

Materials:

copy of storyboard for each student

shoe box decorated to look like a television

picture of a bear from a magazine, the Internet, or one of the books from this unit

tape

scissors

crayons

Directions:

1. Make two slits along the sides of the shoe box to fit the storyboard (see illustration below). Be sure the slits are wide enough to pull the storyboards through easily.

2. Select a picture of a bear and tape it to the chalkboard. Discuss this bear with the children, explaining that they will be writing a class story about this bear.

3. Distribute a storyboard to each child. Have children draw a picture of the bear doing some activity. Ask each student to tell you what the bear is doing, and write it on his/her storyboard. Cut out the storyboard.

4. When all children have completed their storyboards and received assistance in writing about the bear, tape all the storyboards together. The taped storyboards will be pulled through the shoe box, one after another. (You may choose to cut blank story boards out and tape them together to show students a sample of how this is to be done.)

5. Brainstorm a title for this story. Design a storyboard for the title page of the class story.

6. Gather students around to watch the class bear story. Pull the storyboards through the slits in the shoe box and read them one at a time. Students will be excited to see their contribution to the class bear story!

Touch the Sky, My Little Bear

by David Bedford

Summary

This beautiful picture book is set in the Arctic where polar bears live. This is a story of a young polar bear full of questions. Just out of infancy, he asks his mother, "What is it like to be big?" His patient mother shows him what to expect as he grows—how he will one day run like the wind, jump as high as a bird, and dive and swim like a fish. He will be so tall that he will almost touch the sky! In the Arctic world, the polar bear has a different way of life than the brown or black bear. The mother bear educates her new polar bear cub. The pictures and the relationship between the mother and the new cub are lovely.

Sample Plan

Day 1

- Discuss the differences between polar bears and other bears.
- Read *Touch the Sky, My Little Bear* to the class.
- Discuss what students have learned about polar bears.
- Have students color and cut out the picture puzzle of the polar bear (page 24).
- Read about and discuss famous bears (page 34).

Day 2

- Practice number order by doing the "Before and After" math activity (page 40).
- Have students do the "Fishing for Food" activity (page 25).
- Select some bear songs and finger plays to do as a class (page 58).
- Make "Bear-y Yummy Treats" (pages 61–62).
- Select bear art activities to complete (pages 53–56).

Day 3

- Read *Touch the Sky, My Little Bear* to the class again.
- Have students make their own polar bears with the "Cotton Ball Polar Bears." (page 26).

- Find items and words in the classroom that begin with a **B**. Complete "It Starts with a **B**..." (Page 36).
- Have students make their "Bear Counting Books" (pages 41–43).

Day 4

- Discuss the differences between the students and polar bears. Complete the "Us and the Bear" activity (page 52).
- Have students do the "Polar Bear Maze" activity (page 27).
- Select bear art activities to complete (pages 53–56).
- Assemble the "My Bear Book" with students. Read through their books together (pages 48–51).
- Review the bear facts by playing the "Bear Matching Game" (page 69).

Day 5

- Read other stories about polar bears (check your local library and the bibliography on page 79 for suggestions).
- Select "Bear-y Fun Games" to play with students (page 57).
- Organize and play the "Bear Adventure Game" (pages 63–66).

Overview of Activities

Setting the Stage

1. Set up the activities, awards, door handles, and other materials described in the Unit Management section (page 70.)

2. Ask students the following questions prior to reading the story:

   What is the difference between a polar bear and a brown or black bear?

   What does a polar bear eat?

   Where does a polar bear live and sleep?

   What else do you know about polar bears?

3. Talk with students about their mothers. What do mothers do? What do you like about your mother? What are some questions that you ask your mother? Tell students that this is a story about a polar bear cub and his mother.

4. Gather students together in a circle and show them the cover of the book *Touch the Sky, My Little Bear.* Talk about the cover. Have students share predictions of what they think the book will be about. Ask students to be listening for the answers to the questions you just asked.

Enjoying the Book

1. Read the book *Touch the Sky, My Little Bear* aloud to students. Be sure to spend plenty of time looking at the pictures, and encourage students to ask questions. After the book has been read, ask students to share what they liked about the book. What did they learn about polar bears from this book? Do they know any more information about polar bears that was not in the book?

2. Have available a basket of different books about polar bears. Read a few books from the basket and compare these stories. How are they alike? How are they different?

3. Set up a center where students can go to listen to the books that have been recorded onto cassette tapes. (See page 29 for ideas.) Be sure to have available both nonfiction and fiction books about polar bears.

4. Do the "Polar Bear Maze" activity on page 27 and the "Fishing for Food" activity on page 25. Have students color and cut out the "Picture Puzzle" on page 24.

5. Design and incorporate activities based on bears and teddy bears into the classroom. Math, reading, science, art, and life skills lessons and activities correlate with *Touch the Sky, My Little Bear.*

6. Assemble "My Bear Book" ahead of time for students. Make copies of pages 48–51 for each student. Cut out the pages. Stack the reproduced pages one (top) to six (bottom). Line up the left edges of all sheets; staple them along the edge to create a spine.

Overview of Activities *(cont.)*

Extending the Book

1. After finishing the story *Touch the Sky, My Little Bear*, have students write or tell another story about bears. Compare this story with the other two core stories that you have previously read in this unit. What are the similarities and differences? Have students write their own polar bear stories. Compile these pages into a Big Book that can be placed in the class library. The title of this book might be *Polar Bears One, Two, Three*, or you may choose to come up with another title as a class.

2. Select unfamiliar words from the story. Write these words and teach students their meanings. Use them in a sentence. Point out these words when they are used in conversation or in other books.

3. Search for information about the author and illustrator of this book. If possible, read other books by this same author or illustrator. Read the book *Polar Bear, Polar Bear, What do you Hear?* by Eric Carle (see the Bibliography on page 79). Read other books about polar bears.

4. Watch movies from your school library about polar bears.

5. Have the students read "round robin" stories about a polar bear (page 28 for more information). Another fun activity is the story chain described on page 28. The story chain activity will help students remember the sequence of a story.

6. Using a globe or a map, show students where the Arctic is. Show the distance between the Arctic and the state in which you are located. Explain that the Arctic is very cold. Discuss with students what humans would need to wear, eat, and do to survive in the Arctic.

7. Select art activities that you would like to complete as a class (pages 53–56). Don't forget to use the bear awards on page 74 to spread confidence and encouragement in your class.

8. Select and cook the recipes on pages 61–62. Discuss the differences between the food we eat and the food that bears eat. Then discuss the similarities.

Picture Puzzle

Color the picture of the polar bear below. When you are finished, cut along the lines of the picture to create a puzzle. Put the puzzle of the polar bear together. You can store the puzzle pieces in an envelope or plastic bag.

Fishing for Food

Polar bears have to hunt for food. They hunt for walrus and seals. Different bears hunt for different types of food. Provide students with pictures of the kinds of foods bears eat. While students are out of the classroom, hide the different pictures of food throughout your classroom. Later, ask the students to pretend to be bears looking for their food. The "bear" who finds the most food is the winner. (Be sure to make duplicate copies of this page so that there are enough food items for all the "bears" to find.)

Cotton Ball Polar Bears

Make a copy of the bear shape below on cardstock paper for each student. Have students glue on cotton balls to make their own polar bears. You can glue on pieces of felt to make eyes and a mouth.

Polar Bear Maze

Help the polar bear find his way down off the iceberg. Color the picture using crayons or markers.

Language Arts Activities

Hide-a-Book Treasure Hunt

Hide books about bears throughout your classroom. These can be fiction or nonfiction books. Inform students that you will be going on a book treasure hunt. Have children look for the first book. As soon as it is found, sit down and read it. All of the children in your class must gather in a circle to read the book wherever it was found. After the book has been found, send children off to find the next book. Find and read this book in its new location. This can be a fun experience. Be sure to hide a book under a table, by the door, or in another unusual place. Books can even be hidden outside if the weather permits.

Basket o' Books

Keep a basket of books about bears in your classroom. Allow children a chance to peruse these books during free reading time. Once a day, select a book from the basket and read it aloud to the students. At the end of the book, ask the question, "Is it make believe or real?" Discuss with children the difference between a book about a real bear and a pretend bear. Make separate piles of make believe and real books.

Story Chains

After you have read a book about bears, invite each child to contribute to a story chain. Have each child tell you one thing that happened in the story, and write each individual response on a different strip of construction paper. Staple each strip together in the order that the story occurred to create a chain. Read each link in the chain aloud. Hang the story chain in a prominent place in your classroom. This activity will aid students in comprehension skills and help them to recall events that happen in a story.

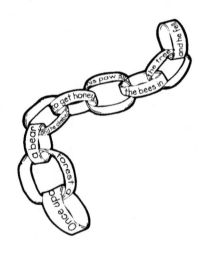

Round Robin Stories

Have children sit in a large circle around an object. (This object can be a teddy bear or another item that is related to bears.) Explain to the children that you will be telling a story as a class. Begin a story about the object in the center of the circle. Once you have a good introduction, ask the child sitting next to you to explain what happens next. This child should add a sentence or two to the story. Continue in this fashion, giving each child a turn to contribute to the story. You will most likely get some giggles and laughs as the story expands. (Another fun technique is to record this activity on a cassette tape, and then make plans to listen to the story again later. Children love to hear themselves on tape.) This activity helps students to understand the components of a story.

Puppetry and Plays

Have props and puppets available for different stories that you plan to read to your class. Students will love to act out the stories as you read them. They will remember the stories better when they have a visual image of the characters in action! You are sure to get some laughs as the students enjoy the antics of the actors and actresses.

Language Arts Activities *(cont.)*

Listening Center

Record readings of a variety of books about bears. Keep the cassette tapes next to the books. At a specific time, have students use headphones to listen to the stories and follow along in the books. You might ask a classroom of older students to read the stories onto cassette tapes.

Class Bear

Bring a teddy bear to class (or make the teddy bear on pages 76–78). This bear will remain in the classroom for the duration of the thematic unit on bears. Involve the class bear in as many ways as you can. Spend time as a class brainstorming and selecting a name for the bear. Read a story to the children using the teddy bear's made-up voice. Place a book in the teddy bear's lap before students come in each morning. The children will be excited to see which book will be read each day. Have students write stories about adventures with the class bear. Have the class teddy bear write letters to the children. Allow time for the children to "write" letters back and draw pictures for the teddy bear. Be creative. Let the children think of ways to involve the class bear, as well.

Brainstorming the Bear

Using the class teddy bear (or the students' own teddy bears), brainstorm different words that can be used to describe the teddy bear. Write these words on a large piece of paper. This technique will help students learn to brainstorm, and it can act as a vocabulary booster as well. Brainstorm words for a variety of different bears. Discuss the differences and similarities with the students. You can also put up magazine pictures of bears to use as a brainstorming tool.

Bear Paw Trail of Books

Foster the love of reading by making a bear trail in the classroom. Cut out bear paws (page 56). Each time you read a book as a class, write the title and author of the book on a paw and staple it on the classroom wall. Your students will be amazed as the trail of bear paws gets longer and longer.

The Big B Hunt

Write the word *bear* on the chalkboard or in another prominent place in your classroom. Discuss the fact that bear starts with the letter *B*. Ask children if there are other words that start with the letter *B*. Each time the children see or find a word that begins with *B*, add it to the list. You may choose to make this a homework assignment. Add words to the list as students bring them in.

Beary Special Students

Select one student each day to be the "Beary Special Student." Have classmates help write positive comments and compliments about the student on the chalkboard. Let the class bear sit on this student's desk or near his/her chair. As a treat, you could even give this special student a bag of gummy bears.

Daily Language Experience

Since whole language encompasses speaking, listening, reading and writing, it is important to include all of these as part of the daily program. Below are prompts that can be used for daily language experiences. During the discussion, the teacher should record student responses or let the students write their response in the Bear Shaped Journal (pages 31–32).

You may choose to create bulletin boards using student responses to the following topics:

1. If I were a bear, I would...
2. If I were a bear, the first thing I would do after winter would be to...
3. Bears have sharp claws to...
4. Bears have fur coats to...
5. If I were walking through the woods and saw a grizzly bear, I would...
6. A bear is scary because...
7. Smokey the Bear says...
8. One day I lost my teddy bear and...
9. I like my teddy bear because...
10. It makes me feel good to sleep with my teddy because...
11. Once when we were camping, I saw a bear and...
12. Bears need heavy fur because...
13. If I wanted to see a real bear, I'd...
14. Bears use their paws to...
15. It's not safe to make friends with a real bear because...
16. What do bears do for fun?
17. What would you tell people if you were a bear?
18. Describe the perfect teddy bear.
19. If you were a bear, what would you pack for your long winter's hibernation?
20. If you were a bear, what would you do to get ready for a long winter's hibernation?
21. A bear's favorite meal is...
22. What is the name of your teddy bear?
23. A teddy bear makes a good friend because...
24. What should you do if you ever see a bear?
25. Bears are amazing animals because...

The following questions should be asked after you have read all the books featured in this unit:

1. Eddie loves playing with the big bear because...
2. What would you name the big bear?
3. What would you name the big bear's teddy bear?
4. What do the big bear and Eddie do for fun?
5. Bears like to eat...
6. Bears like to sleep in...
7. Little Polar Bear is...
8. Polar Bears live where it is...
9. Bears can be different colors, such as...
10. I think learning about bears is...

Bear Shaped Journal

Reproduce the bear cover onto construction paper (white, yellow, black or brown). Students can add color and personality with crayons or markers. They should write their name on the cover and cut it out.

Bear Shaped Journal *(cont.)*

Duplicate enough of these lined pages for each child to include several in his/her own journal. Use with Daily Language Experience activities on page 30.

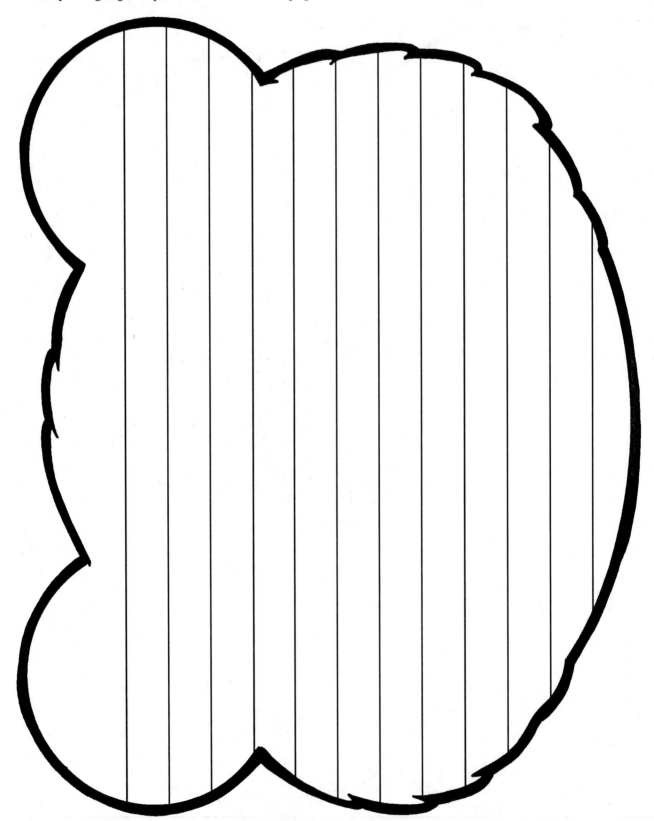

Letter to Teddy

Write a letter to your teddy bear. What do you want to tell him or her? Be sure to give your letter to your teddy.

Famous Bears

There are many bears with whom students may be familiar. Spend time discussing the pretend and real characteristics of these famous bears. Some helpful and informative websites are listed below.

Smokey the Bear

Smokey the Bear is the mascot for fire safety. Check out books on fire safety and invite a firefighter to come and talk to your class about fire safety tips. Discuss why Smokey the Bear might be concerned about fire safety. You might check to see if Smokey the Bear can visit your classroom. Use the websites below to download activity pages on Smokey the Bear.

http://www.smokeybear.com/

The official Smokey the Bear website

http://r05s001.pswfs.gov/stanislaus/kidcenter/activity.htm

Smokey the Bear activity pages for kids

Berenstain Bears

The Berenstain Bears are well-known for their antics and stories. Jan and Stan Berenstain have written many children's books on a variety of topics. Though their bears are not real, they can still be used to reinforce concepts you may be trying to teach in your classroom. Be sure to discuss the difference between real and pretend bears. You may wish to compare a picture of a real bear with a picture of the Berenstain Bears.

http://villa.lakes.com/mariska/bears/

Lesson plan ideas, activity pages and more about the Berenstain Bears

http://www.berenstainbears.com/

The official Berenstain Bears website

Corduroy

Corduroy is another favorite bear to read about. Read the stories about Corduroy to your students. *Corduroy*, by Don Freeman (Viking Press, 1976) and *Pocket for Corduroy* (Viking Press, 1980) are both good selections to read to your class. Perhaps you can even find a teddy bear that looks similar to Corduroy.

Paddington the Bear

The book *A Bear Called Paddington* (Houghton Mifflin, 1998) was written by Michael Bond. This lovable bear has an official website with information and activities for children.

http://www.paddingtonbear.com.uk/

Winnie the Pooh

Another famous and favorite bear is Winnie the Pooh. You may choose to bring in stuffed animals of all the characters from this famous series of books. Allow children to hold and play with the animals while you read a Winnie the Pooh story to them. See Bibliography on page 79 for suggestions.

http://www.electrontrap.org/jmilne/Pooh/

Poetry Pizzazz

There are many fun poetry activities that can be used when you are learning about bears. Use the poems and activities below to enrich your study of bears.

Acrostic Poems

Write a word for each letter of the word bear. See how many different variations your students can create. You might choose to use other bear-related words such as berries, hibernation, honey, or cave to create more acrostic poems. Below is a sample acrostic:

Big
Eats berries and acorns
Ants are yummy!
Runs fast!

Pattern Poetry

Use the well-known book *Polar Bear, Polar Bear, What do you see?* by Eric Carle (page 79 of bibliography) to create pattern poetry. Students recite the first line of the book and create a subsequent line of their own. They can then illustrate their pattern poem. Put the poems together to create a class book. Store the book in the class library for all students to read.

Poetic Rhyming Words

Select a word to begin with. Have students find words that rhyme with this word and make a sentence together. Below is a sample:

BIG (Big is the original word.)
The bear is <u>big</u>!
The bear wears a <u>wig</u>.
The bear dances a <u>jig</u>.
The bear eats a <u>fig</u>.
The bear is a <u>pig</u>!

Pocket Poetry

Have children write words that describe their teddy bears. Help them design a poem using these words. Once the poem is written out, fold it up and put the poem in the pocket of their teddy bear's clothes or on its lap.

Read Aloud Poetry

Find poems in the library to read to your students. The rhyming sounds of the words are pleasing to children and can demonstrate rhythm and poetry. Display poetry books in your classroom so that students may read them during free reading time.

It Starts with a B . . .

Draw a line from the bear to each of the pictures that starts with the letter **B**.
Color.

Homework Tip: Have students go home and cutout pictures that start with a **B** from magazines and newspapers. Then they may bring the pictures to school for classroom sharing.

Bear Counters

Count the number of bears in each group. Circle the correct number.

1.   3   4   5

2.   2   1   3

3.   4   5   3

4.   5   6   7

Extension: Read the book *Let's Count it Out, Jesse Bear,* by Nancy White Carlstrom with your students (see bibliography on page 79). The book will provide children with practice in counting and reviewing numbers.

Grin and Bear It

Connect the dots by counting from 1 to 20. Color the picture.

Match the Bears

Color the bears using the color code.

Color Code	
Brown 1	Blue 4
Red 2	Black 5
Yellow 3	Green 6

Before and After

Write the number that comes before each number below.

_____ 3   _____ 4

_____ 9   _____ 10

_____ 2   _____ 8

_____ 5   _____ 7

_____ 7   _____ 6

Write the number that comes after each number below.

5 _____   8 _____

1 _____   9 _____

7 _____   6 _____

3 _____   2 _____

4 _____   10 _____

Write the number that comes between each number below.

4 _____ 6   1 _____ 3   3 _____ 5

Bear Counting Book

Directions:

Make your own bear counting book using the next few pages.

1. Cut along the lines of each page. Staple the pages together in numerical order.

2. Cut two squares of construction paper to fit this book. Use these squares as a cover.

3. Have children color pictures or use stamps or stickers to create the number of bears for each page. The number of bears should correspond with the number printed on each page. (Another option is to cut bear shapes out of sponges and allow students to sponge paint bears on each page.)

4. When children have completed their pages, staple them all together with the covers to create the finished product.

5. Allow each child a chance to read his/her book to another student. Be sure to send the book home for the child to share it with his/her family!

1 bear

2 bears

Bear Counting Book *(cont.)*

3 bears	**5 bears**
4 bears	**6 bears**

Bear Counting Book *(cont.)*

7 bears

9 bears

8 bears

10 bears

Virtual Zoos

Though you may live far from a zoo, you can still access pictures of real bears on the Internet. Listed below are websites that feature virtual zoos and pictures of a variety of bears.

http://www.ccsd.net/schools/brown/zoo/main.html

Brown Junior High School Virtual Zoo—Information on the brown bear, North American black bear, polar bear, sun bear, spectacled bear, and the sloth bear.

http://www.channel4000.com/partners/mnzoo/sunbear.html

Minnesota Zoo—Check out the pictures and information on the sun bear.

http://www.primenet.com/~brendel/ursidae.html

Cyber Zoo Mobile—Information and pictures on different species of bears.

http://www.lpzoo.com/tour/tour.html

Lincoln Park Zoo—Information and pictures on the spectacled and sun bear.

http://www.aza.org/gallery/index.cfm

American Zoo Association Photo Gallery—check out photo of spectacled bear.

http://home.earthlink.net/~bruno6/

Pictures of different types of bears.

http://www.nature-net.com/bears/ and http://www.nature-net.com/bears/readers.html

Facts and information on different types of bears.

Roll-a-Bear

Materials:

paper for each child

one crayon for each child

one die per group of three or four children

Directions:

1. Once students have an idea of how a bear looks, you are ready to play the game "Roll a Bear." Divide students into groups of three or four.

2. Give each child a piece of paper and a crayon. Give each group a die. Each child takes a turn rolling the die.

3. Depending on what number is rolled, a certain part of the bear is drawn. (Draw a picture of the key below on the chalkboard.) The first child to draw a complete bear is the winner. If a child rolls the number of a bear part that is already drawn, then no other bear "parts" are added.

Key	
1 = bear head	4 = two bear arms
2 = bear ears	5 = two bear legs
3 = bear tummy	6 = bear eyes, nose, mouth

Bear Habitat

Materials:

- A piece of paper for each child, folded to make four squares.
- crayons
- paper plates
- clay or craft dough

Directions:

Just how does a bear live? Using books that give accurate information about bears, have children draw pictures of how bears eat, sleep, and play. Then using clay, have students make a clay bear and a clay habitat. Students might make a cave for the bear to live in. They might create fish, berries, and other foods for the bear to eat, and other items that are associated with bears. When students have finished, they can place their clay figures and items on a paper plate to dry.

Craft Dough

2 cups (500 mL) flour
1 cup (250 mL) salt
2 Tablespoons (25 mL) oil

1 Teaspoon (5 mL) food coloring (optional)
2 cups (500 mL) water

Directions:

Combine all ingredients and mix well. Store in an airtight plastic container.

How Big is a Bear?

Cut out different-sized ovals to show how big the different types of bears are. Hang these ovals in your classroom. Make a list of things that are bigger than and smaller than a bear.

- A **black bear** weighs about 130–660 pounds (58,968–299,374 kg) and is 50–75"(128–192 cm) in length.

- A **polar bear** weighs 440–1760 pounds (199,583–798,331 kg) and is about 8'5" (259 cm) in length.

- A **grizzly bear** weighs 300–860 pounds (136,079–390,093 kg) and is about 9'6" (292 cm) in length.

Use the following website for more facts and information on bears:

http://www.ameritech.net/users/macler/bears.html#RealBears

Classifying and Sorting

The day your students bring their teddy bears to share with the class, teach this lesson on classification. There are a variety of different ways to classify and sort teddy bears. Be sure to complete only one category at a time.

Students should physically move their teddy bear into the right group, based on what classification is designated. Some classifications will have several groups, while others will have only two groups in which students may place their bears. The teacher will call out the first group (i.e., "brown bears"), and all students with brown bears will place their bears in a designated spot. Then all the black bears will be placed in a group, and the rest of the bears will be placed in the corresponding group.

Use the following classification suggestions as a guide:

- What is the size?
- What is the color?
- What is the shape?
- What is the stuffing?
- Does the teddy bear wear a bow, hat, or other item?
- What is the texture of the teddy bear? (Soft, smooth, scratchy, hard, rough, etc.)
- Is the teddy bear old or new?
- Is the teddy bear male or female?
- Is the teddy bear real or pretend?
- Was the teddy bear a gift, or did you pick it out?
- Is the teddy bear handmade or bought in a store?
- Is the teddy bear your friend or just a bear/stuffed animal?
- Where does the teddy bear live? (On the bed, on the shelf, on the dresser, etc.)
- Does the teddy bear have a name? (First? Last? Middle?)
- Does the teddy bear have a nickname?
- Is this the only teddy bear at home, or does this bear have other friends there?
- Does the teddy bear have moveable arms and/or legs?

Be sure to ask students for suggestions regarding how these bears can be classified. You may be surprised at the ideas they have!

What do Bears Eat?

Cut and paste into the box only the foods that bears eat.

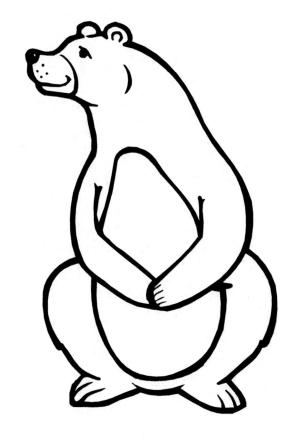

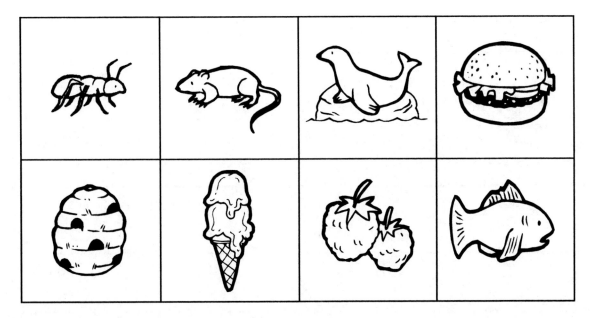

My Bear Book

My Bear Book

Name _____ 1

I have read my bear book with:

_____

_____

_____

_____

2

My Bear Book *(cont.)*

Black bears are the smallest bears. Black bears can climb trees. Black bears eat berries, honey, grass, and other foods. Mother bears take care of their cubs.

3

The Black Bear

4

My Bear Book (cont.)

Grizzly bears have brown fur with silver tips. Grizzly bears have small eyes, round ears, a short tail, and a hump on their shoulders. Grizzly bears hibernate all winter and wake up very hungry in the spring.

5

The Grizzly Bear

6

My Bear Book *(cont.)*

Polar bears live near the North Pole. They have yellowish-white fur. They have a long neck and a narrow head. Most polar bears do not sleep in the winter. They have thick fur to keep warm. They hunt walrus, seals, and birds.

7

The Polar Bear

8

Us and the Bear

How are people similar to bears? How are we different than bears? Draw pictures of things that are the same in the oval. Draw pictures of things that are different in the rectangle.

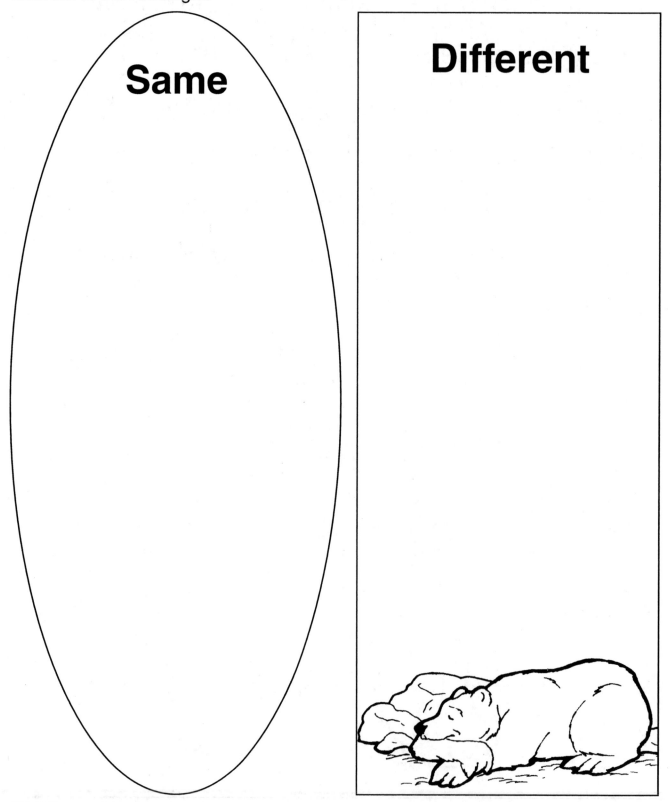

Same

Different

52

Amazing Art Activities

Use the following art activities to reinforce eye-hand coordination as well as the skills of coloring, gluing, painting, and cutting with scissors. You can also use these projects to decorate your classroom!

Note: Many of these activities require more adult assistance than one person can provide. Plan ahead to have parents or other helpers aid in the creation of these art activities.

Glue

- Paper Bag Puppet—Use the pattern on page 54 to make a bear puppet. Have students color the pattern, then cut it out. Ask students to glue the bear face onto the paper bag. Be sure to make a sample ahead of time for students to use as a guide.

Paint and Chalk

- Bear Sponges—Trace the bear figure on page 54 on a sponge and cut it out for painting. Give students large pieces of white paper on which to sponge paint their bears. You can use these paintings as wrapping paper for a gift created in the classroom.

- Sidewalk Chalk—If weather permits, give sidewalk chalk to students. Have them draw a mural of a bear in his home. Students can draw a forest, a cave, snow, the sun, berries, and anything else they can think of that would appear near their bear.

Paper

- Paper Placemat—For the teddy bear picnic, you can have students make a quick and easy placemat. Use scissors to cut pieces of construction paper into one-inch strips. Be sure to use a variety of colors. Each child should have several strips of different-colored construction paper. Fold a large piece of construction paper in half lengthwise for each child. Starting at the fold, cut slits across the paper lengthwise. Leave about an inch uncut at the edge of the paper. Show students how to weave strips of paper in and out of the slits—first over one slit, then under the next, through to the other side. Repeat with the next slit, starting under the slit, then going over. Alternate each strip until the placemat is finished.

- Paper Plate Bear Mask—For this activity, make a copy of the bear face on page 55 for each student. Let them color their face and glue it onto a paper plate. Help them cut holes for eyes. Then staple a cardboard tube to the bottom of the mask to use as a handle. Have students act out bear stories.

- Teddy Bear Paper Dolls—Use brown, yellow, or white paper to cut a string of teddy bear dolls. Fold the paper lengthwise in fourths. Use a pencil to draw the shape of a teddy bear on the top fold. Make sure the teddy bear touches folds on both sides. Use scissors to cut out the figure, keeping the folded edges intact in several places on the drawing. Open the paper for a row of teddy bears. Have students illustrate their teddy bears with crayons or markers.

Bear Patterns

Bear Patterns *(cont.)*

Bear Patterns *(cont.)*

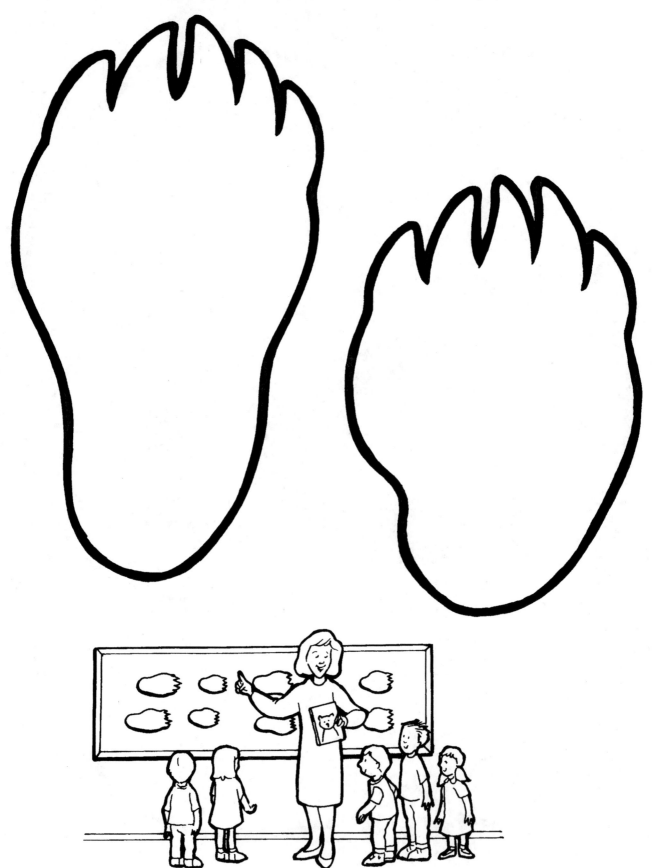

Bear-y Fun Games

There are many physical activities that you can do which involve bears. These experiences can get out the wiggles at the beginning of the day, or act as a transition between two quiet activities. Select one or more of the following activities to do as a class:

Hot and Cold

Select a student to step out of the classroom. Have remaining students help you hide the bear. Ask the student to return to the classroom. He/she then looks for the hidden teddy bear. The students give clues by saying, "Hot, hotter, or hottest" whenever the student gets close to the bear. Students can also say, "Cold, colder, coldest" when the searching student is far from the hidden bear.

Teddy Bear!

Arrange students in a circle. This game is played similarly to Duck, Duck Goose. Select one student to be *It*. The person who is *It* walks around and taps the head of each student in the circle. As *It* walks around the circle tapping heads, he/she selects five students and says, "Teddy." *It* returns to his/her spot, and the five students must be ready and listening for when the student who is *It* says, "TEDDY BEAR!" Upon hearing the words, "TEDDY BEAR," the five students who were selected race around the circle and go back to their starting position. There they stand quietly, holding very still. The first student who gets back to his/her place and stands quietly is *It* next.

The Bouncy Bear

This game requires a parachute or a large sheet. Have students hang onto the edges of the sheet or the parachute. Begin with one teddy bear placed in the middle of the parachute. Toss the bear up and down using the parachute or sheet. You can review numbers (or the ABCs) by counting as the bear is tossed in the air. You can also place teddy bears under the parachute and instruct students to run in, forming a tent with them and the teddy bears inside.

Hot Teddy

Have students sit in a circle. A teddy bear acts as a "hot potato." Students pass the teddy bear. Keep your back to the circle as students pass the teddy around. When you turn around, and say "Hot!" whoever is holding or touching the teddy bear is "out." Play continues this way until only one student is left. When students get out, they can cheer and help judge who has the teddy when the teacher says "hot."

Teddy ABCs

Have students sit in a circle. Work on eye-hand coordination by tossing and catching the teddy bear as it circulates around. As a student catches the teddy, he/she must say the letter that comes next as ABCs are chanted. (You can chant numbers, as well.)

Bear Songs and Finger Plays

Five Little Bears
(To the tune of "Five Little Monkeys")

Five little bears were sleeping in their cave.
(Make snoring sounds and put hands up to head like a pillow.)
One woke up and scratched his little head.
(Scratch your head)
Mama Bear was snoring, then sleepily said,
"Please don't wake up; just stay in your bed!"
(Make snoring sound, and then shake your finger)
Four little bears... (and so on)
Three little bears... (and so on)
Two little bears...(and so on)
One little bear was sleeping in his cave.
He woke up and scratched his little head.
Mama Bear was snoring; then the little one said,
"Please wake up Mama! We're ready to be fed!"
(Rub your tummy like you are hungry.)

Two Big Black Bears
(To the tune of "Two Little Bluebirds")

Two big Black bears, sitting on a hill.
One named Blackie, the other named Bill.
(Bring one thumb from behind back at a time. One thumb is Blackie. One thumb is Bill.)
Run away, Blackie.
Run away, Bill.
(Have thumbs run behind your back.)
Come back, Blackie.
Come back, Bill.
(Make growling sound and move thumbs around like two bear cubs playing.)

The Great Big Bear
*(Sing this finger play after you have read **Goldilocks and the Three Bears** to the children.)*

A great big bear,
(Hold hands far apart)
A middle-sized bear,
(Hold hands closer together)
A little bear I see.
(Make a small ball with fingers)
Let's count them all together—
One, Two, Three!
(Students hold up fingers—one, two three!)

Quiet Time Teddy

Option A: Make an enlarged copy of the bear pattern on heavy cardstock paper. Glue on fake fur to cover the body of the bear. Use buttons for eyes and red felt for mouth. Using fabric and a hot glue gun, glue on a jacket that zips and buttons, and shoes with laces to tie. You may choose to make more than one of these teddy bears. Allow time for students to practice the skills of tying shoes, zipping or buttoning up the coat, etc.

Option B: Enlarge the bear pattern and trace it onto black, brown, or white felt. Use the bear clothing patterns to trace clothes onto different colored pieces of felt. Cut out the felt teddy bear and its clothes. Use during class play and story time.

Quiet Time Teddy's Clothes

Use these patterns to make clothes for the felt teddy bear.

Bear-y Yummy Treats

Be aware of food allergies that students may have before making any of the recipes on this page. You may need to alter recipes to include substitute ingredients.

Cranberry Muffins

A hungry bear will eat almost anything—spring flowers, juicy beetles, ants, acorns, and berries of all types. Enjoy a taste of cranberries in this muffin recipe. (You can substitute blueberries or bananas for the cranberries.)

- 1 egg
- ³/₄ (180 L) cup milk
- 1 cup (250 mL) dried cranberry halves
- ¹/₂ tablespoon (15 mL) grated orange peel
- ¹/₂ cup (120 mL) vegetable oil

- 2 cups (500 mL) flour
- ¹/₃ cup (85 mL) sugar
- 3 teaspoons (15 mL) baking powder
- 1 teaspoon salt (5 mL)

Heat oven to 400 degrees. Set paper muffin cups inside muffin tins. Beat egg; stir in milk, oil, cranberries, and orange peel. Stir in remaining ingredients all at once, just until flour is moistened (batter will be lumpy). Fill muffin cups ¹/₂ full. Sprinkle tops of muffins with sugar before baking. Bake until golden brown, about 20 minutes. Immediately remove from pan. Makes one dozen muffins.

Trail Mix with Nuts and Berries

Bears love to eat berries of all types. This is a trail mix recipe which uses dried cranberries. You can add other dried berries and fruit for variation. What might bears add to this trail mix?

- 1 cup (250 mL) peanuts
- 1 cup raisins (250 mL)
- 1 cup dried cranberries (250 mL)

- 1 cup sunflower seeds (250 mL)
- ¹/₂ cup (125 mL) coconut

Mix all ingredients together and serve. (There are a variety of other ingredients that can be added to this tasty treat. Examples include cereal, marshmallows, chocolate chips, pretzels, walnuts, almonds, dried bananas, and dried apples.)

Bear-y Yummy Treats *(cont.)*

Honey Taffy Candy

Another favorite food for bears is honey. Bears steal honey from beehives. The bee stings don't hurt bears because their fur is so thick.

- 1 cup (240 mL) sugar
- $\frac{1}{2}$ cup (120 mL) light corn syrup
- $\frac{1}{2}$ cup (120 mL) honey

- a pinch of cream of tarter
- 2 tablespoons (30 mL) butter
- 1 teaspoon vinegar (5 mL)

Put the sugar, syrup, and honey in a pot. Heat until the sugar dissolves, then add the cream of tartar and boil, stirring constantly, for about 20 minutes. Add the vinegar and butter and let it boil, then pour into a buttered pan. Cool, pull, and cut. (Be sure the candy has cooled enough before allowing children to pull it. Remember to have children wash their hands thoroughly before handling the candy.) Wrap taffy in wax paper. You can add other flavorings and food colorings for variety.

Honey-Bran Muffins

- 1 cup (250 mL) unbleached flour
- $\frac{1}{4}$ teaspoon (1.25 mL) salt
- 1 teaspoon (5 mL) baking soda
- 1 cup (250 mL) bran
- 1 cup (250 mL) buttermilk

- 1 large egg
- $\frac{1}{3}$ cup (83 mL) honey melted with 3 tablespoons butter
- $\frac{1}{2}$ cup (125 mL) diced apples

Preheat over to 350 degrees. Sift together flour, salt and baking soda into a large bowl. Stir in bran. Make a well in the center. Beat together the liquid ingredients. Pour them into the well in the dry mixture. Add apples, and stir just long enough to combine. Fill muffin cups $\frac{2}{3}$ full. Bake 25–30 minutes. Makes 12 muffins.

Bear Adventure Game

(This game needs to be played in groups of four students.)

Materials:

4 bear playing pieces

4 bear bases

4 bear cubs

6 large square tiles

12 circle path tiles

Assembly

1. Color all the playing pieces. Copy the bear playing pieces cubs, and bases onto cardstock. Cut and laminate to keep these pieces sturdy. Slide the bear playing pieces into the bases so that they stand up.

2. Copy the six large square tiles and 12 circle path tiles onto cardstock or heavy paper. Cut out squares and circles. Laminate all tiles to keep tiles intact.

3. Cut the slits in the bears and bear cubs.

Set Up

1. Make a circle with the 12 circle path tiles. These cards should be face-up.

2. Place the six large square tiles inside the circle of path tiles. The square tiles should be face-down. (Placing the squares in rows makes it easier, and laying them down free-form makes it a bit more challenging.)

Object of the Game

The object of the game is to go around the circle with your bear playing piece, collecting the bear cubs from the backs of the other bears. The bear with all four bear cubs on his/her back is the winner.

Directions:

1. Each student places a bear on the outside circle tile of his/her choice and puts a cub on the bear's back. The first student turns over a square tile inside the circle. If this tile matches the circle tile directly in front of the student's bear playing piece, the bear can move to that square.

2. If the bear is able to move ahead because the square tile and the circle tile match, then the bear can continue in this way until he/she turns over a square tile that does not match the circle tile directly in front of the bear. (This part of the game is similar to the matching game. You are trying to match the square tile with the circle tile directly in front of the bear.)

3. When a bear comes up behind another bear, and it is his/her turn, he/she tries to match the square tile with the circle tile directly in front of the bear he/she is trying to pass. If the tiles match, the bear can "fly over" this bear, take a bear cub from it, and put the cub in the slit on his/her back. The first bear to "fly over" and take each bear's cub is the winner.

Bear Adventure Game *(cont.)*

Note: Color each cub to match its corresponding bear.

Bear Stands

Bear Adventure Game *(cont.)*

Bear Adventure Game *(cont.)*

This page needs to be copied *twice.* You will need 12 circle tiles

66

Teddy Bear Picnic

Before Class Preparation

1. Have a teddy bear picnic with the students' teddy bears, and make it a surprise! Hide the students' teddy bears in a secluded area. Spread a blanket on the ground and place each of the teddy bears on the blanket. Next to each teddy bear, put the placemat made by the student (page 53). Students will go on a treasure hunt to find their teddy bears, and then have a picnic.

2. Gather a collection of stories about teddy bears (see the bibliography on page 79 for suggestions). After reading the stories, students will go on a treasure hunt to find their teddy bears.

3. Cut out and hide the treasure hunt clues. These clues are pictures of things that you can find in your classroom. Set aside the picture of the first place students will go. This will be the first clue that is given to them. Then place the consecutive clues upon the other items, as directed by the clues. (You may choose to draw picture clues of your own to match your individual circumstances. Remember to draw pictures of items that can be found easily in your classroom.)

4. Get supplies for the picnic. Purchase teddy bear-related foods to eat at the picnic. Remember to purchase napkins and paper cups. Serve water to drink.

Directions:

1. Gather students in a circle. Explain that you would like to read some stories about teddy bears with them. After reading the stories, ask if students would like to have a picnic with their teddy bears.

2. Explain that the teddy bears are having a picnic right now, and they are hoping that the children will come join them. They need to go on a treasure hunt to find the picnicking teddy bears.

3. Give the first clue to the students. The clue should be a picture of an item in the classroom. The second clue should be taped in a visible place on that item. After the students find the second clue, the treasure hunt continues until all the clues have been found. The last clue will lead to the teddy bear picnic.

4. Have students sit by their teddy bear. Set out graham cracker teddies, gummy bears, and other teddy bear-related foods to snack on at the picnic. Cups of water are best, so that sugary drinks will not spill on the teddy bears.

Mural of Memories

Create a class mural showing the information that students have learned about bears. Have students paint a picture of what they learned about bears, both real and pretend.

Option A: Have students paint the picture on a long piece of butcher paper. Allow each student a turn to paint.

Option B: Have students paint their picture on a smaller piece of white construction paper and paste the individual pictures on a large mural.

Here is a list of concepts, facts, and ideas that have been discussed in this unit on Bears. You may discuss these ideas with your students as a review; this discussion will prompt them to think of what to depict in their pictures.

Mural Ideas

Bears are big.

There are different types of bears.

Bears live in forests.

Bears live in a cave.

Most bears sleep all winter.

Bears walk like people.

Bears will eat almost anything.

Bears like to eat ants, honey, berries, acorns, juicy beetles, and other foods.

Bear begins with the letter B.

Bears have fur.

Baby bears drink milk from their mother.

Bears are brown, yellowish, white or black.

Some bears live in a den.

Bears have paws and long, sharp claws.

Bears eat in the fall to get fat.

Some bears can climb trees.

Black bears teach their baby bears how to climb, swim, and hunt for food.

Polar bears live where it is cold.

Polar bears are good swimmers.

Polar bears hunt seals, walruses, and birds.

Polar bears live near the North Pole.

A baby bear is called a cub.

Teddy bears are pretend bears.

Grizzly bears have a hump on their shoulders.

Bear Matching Game

Materials: Copy this page onto cardstock. To keep this game intact, you may choose to laminate the pieces. Cut the squares out and place them face-down. You should make copies of this page for small groups of students.

Directions: Students take turns flipping two cards over at a time. If the cards match, then the student keeps the matching pair and gets another turn. If the cards do not match, the student turns these cards back over face-down, and the next student tries to find a match. Play continues in this manner until all the matches have been found. Players count up the number of matches they were able to find. The player with the most matches wins.

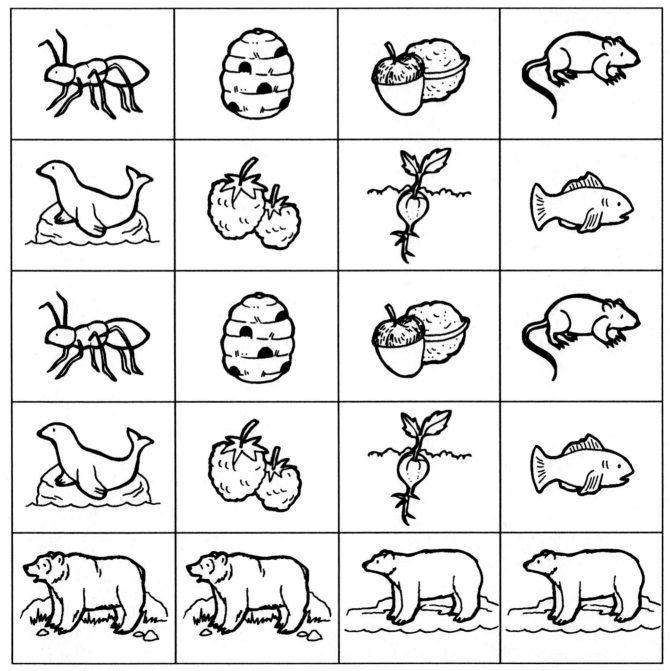

Bear Thematic Unit Skills and Objectives

This is a list of the skills and objectives that are being taught and reinforced as the "Bears Thematic Unit" is studied in the classroom.

Language and Literacy

- Be able to listen to a story and answer questions about it
- Participate in conversations about personally meaningful experiences
- Express oneself and listen to others politely
- Explore and gather information from a variety of sources
- Increase vocabulary
- Identify common objects, places, people, and animals
- Interact with a story: follow along, answer questions, and repeat words
- Tell a story, either made up or repeated
- Write alphabet letters and begin forming words

Visual

- Be aware of the difference between numbers and letters
- Classify and categorize objects

Audio

- Listen to and follow simple instructions
- Express oneself and listen to others
- Participate in simple songs and fingerplays

Math

- Recognize and write numbers 1–10
- Compare attributes (bigger/smaller, shorter/taller)
- Develop awareness of time: old, young, four seasons, yesterday, today

Science

- Expand awareness of the natural world
- Identify types of bears
- Know and understand the seasons

Art

- Cut, paste, color, and paint
- Draw simple shapes

Creative Play

- Be able to role play
- Make models out of craft dough and other materials

Letter to Parents

Dear Parents,

We are about to begin a study of bears. We will be studying real bears, and we will spend some time talking about teddy bears. We will be engaging in bear-related activities that involve cooking, reading, cutting, gluing, writing, thinking, creating, and learning. We will work in learning centers about bears, and we will memorize fingerplays and songs about bears. Math, reading, writing, science, social studies, life skills, art, and physical education will be incorporated in this thematic unit on bears.

If you have any books at home about bears (real or pretend), please read them to your child. This will expand your child's knowledge of bears. Ask your child what he/she is learning about bears in school. You may be amazed at how much your child knows about bears!

There will be a week in which children will be invited to bring a teddy bear from home to share with the class. Please help your child select a teddy bear that would be appropriate to bring to school. (If your child does not have a teddy bear to bring, another special stuffed animal would be acceptable.) Please do not send a teddy bear that is considered fragile. Children will be sitting with their teddy bears, classifying teddy bears, and writing letters, songs, and poems about their teddy bears.

If you would like to help us on cooking day, or assist with any of our art projects, please sign and return the form below. We appreciate any assistance we are given in the classroom!

Sincerely,

_____

- -

Please check the following:

❑ I would be happy to help with art and/or cooking activities in the classroom.

❑ I will not be able to help at this time. Please ask me again in the future to assist in the classroom.

_____
Child's Name

_____   _____
Parent's Name   Phone

Bear Newsletter

The Classroom Newsletter

What We're Learning

Upcoming Events

"Beary Important Kids in the News"

New at School

Bear Door Handles

Cut out the door handles and laminate, if you wish. Hang these on your classroom door.

Bear Awards

Color or copy on colored paper. Cut and give awards to students to encourage them in their efforts. You can allow students to present awards to other students in order to encourage feelings of confidence and accomplishment in your classroom.

To:

You did a "Beary" good job.

From:

To:

#1 Bear Student

From:

To:

Way to Go!

From:

To:

You are so Grrrrrreat!

From:

To:

"Beary" Amazing Work!

From:

To:

Keep up the Grrrrrreat Work!

From:

To:

You are "beary" Special!

From:

To:

You did it with your "bear" hands! Good for you!

From:

Bear Bulletin Boards

Hats off to "Beary" Good Work!

Objective:

This bulletin board can be used to spotlight student work and achievement.

Materials:

- Background paper to cover bulletin board
- Border to surround bulletin board
- Lettering for words on bulletin board

Directions:

1. Put up bulletin board paper, staple the surrounding border, and affix the lettering on bulletin board.
2. Copy bear patterns on pages 76–78 on colored paper, or allow students to color the bears.
3. Staple the bears next to individual student work on the bulletin board.

Real or Pretend?

Objective:

This bulletin board is used to teach the concepts of real and pretend.

Materials:

- Background paper to cover bulletin board
- Border to surround the bulletin board
- Lettering for words on bulletin board
- Strips of paper
- Bears to decorate bulletin board (see patterns on pages 76–78)

Directions:

1. Put up bulletin board paper, staple the surrounding border, and affix the lettering to the bulletin board. Copy bear patterns to decorate the bulletin board.
2. Write sentences on word strips. Some of the sentences need to be about pretend bears and others need to be about real bears. (Pretend examples include: You can sleep with a bear. Bears wear clothes. Bears have teddy bears. A bear lives in a house. Real bear examples include: Bears can fish. Bears can growl. Bears eat berries.)
3. Read each word strip and have students determine whether or not the word strip should go under the pretend heading or the real bear heading. Use the board to inspire a class discussion about the difference between real and pretend.

Class Bear Patterns

See pages 29 and 75 for suggested uses.

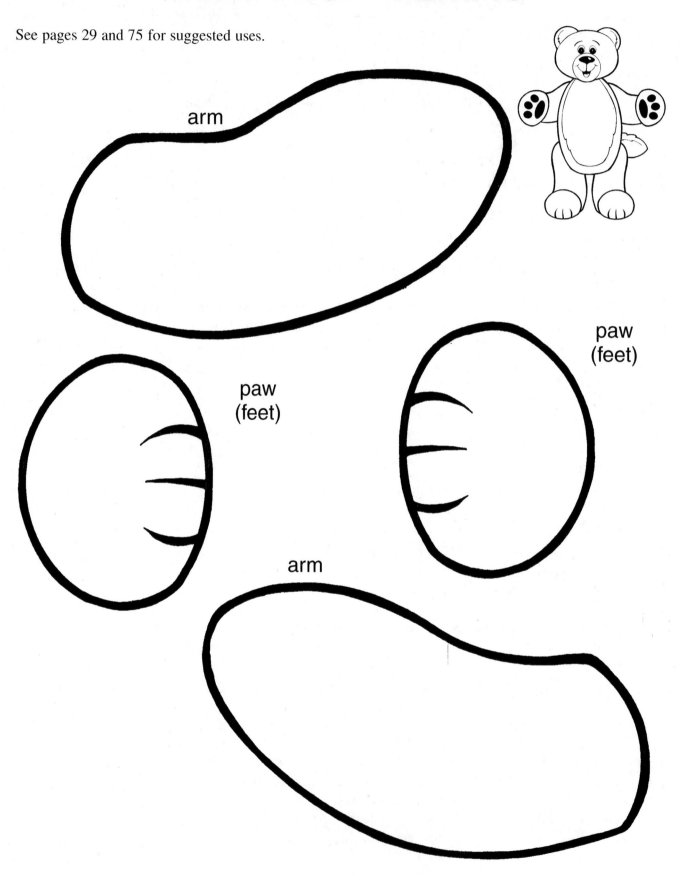

arm

paw
(feet)

paw
(feet)

arm

Class Bear Patterns *(cont.)*

See pages 29 and 75 for suggested uses.

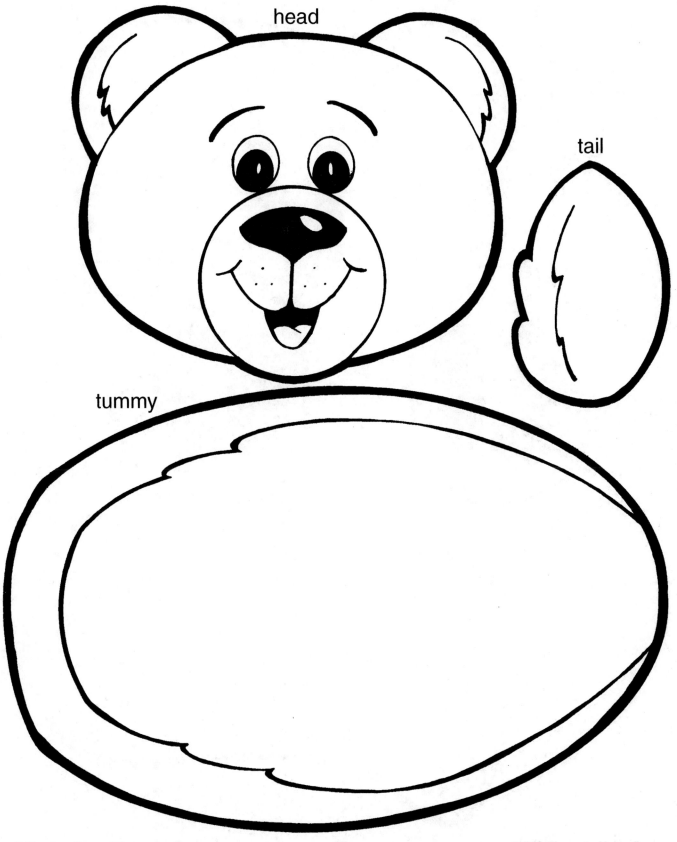

head

tail

tummy

Class Bear Patterns *(cont.)*

See pages 29 and 75 for suggested uses.

leg

front paw

front paw

leg

Bibliography

Core Books

Alborough, Jez. *My Friend Bear*. Candlewick Press, 1998.
Bedford, David. *Touch the Sky, My Little Bear*. Handprint Books, 2001.
Milton, Joyce. *Bears are Curious*. Random House, 1998.

Fiction

Alborough, Jez. *It's the Bear!* Candlewick Press, 1994.
Alborough, Jez. *Where's My Teddy?* Candlewick Press, 1992.
Baldwin, Sherry. *Beecher Bear Plays Here and There*. Read-it-to-Me Publishing, 2000.
Brett, Jan. *Berlioz the Bear*. Paper Star, 1996.
Carle, Eric. *Brown Bear, Brown Bear, What do you See?* Henry Holt & Co., Inc., 1996.
Carle, Eric. *Polar Bear, Polar Bear, What do you Hear?* Henry Holt & Co., Inc., 1997.
Carlstrom, Nancy White. *Happy Birthday, Jesse Bear!* Simon & Schuster, 1994.
Carlstrom, Nancy White. *Let's Count it Out, Jesse Bear*. First Aladdin Paperbacks, 1996.
de Beer, Hans. *Ahoy There, Little Bear*. North South Books, 1999.
de Beer, Hans. *Little Polar Bear*. North South Books, 1999.
Edwards, Richard. *Copy Me, Copycub*. HarperCollins Juvenile Books, 1999.
Fox, Mem. *Sleepy Bears*. Harcourt Brace, 1999.
Kennedy, Jimmy. *Teddy Bear's Picnic*. Peter Bedrick Books, 1990.
Kern, Noris. *I Love You with All My Heart*. Chronicle Books, 1998.
Milne, A. A. *Winnie-the-Pooh*. Dell, 1970.
Rosen, Michael. *We're Going on a Bear Hunt*. Macmillan, 1989.
Seuss, Dr. *The Big Brag*. Random House, 1998.
Turkle, Brinton. *Deep in the Forest*. Dutton, 1987.
Waddell, Martin. *You and Me Little Bear*. Candlewick Press, 1999.

Nonfiction

Fair, Jeff (with photography by Lynn Rogers). *Bears for Kids*. NorthWord Press, 1991.
Gill, Shelley. *Alaska's Three Bears*. Paws IV Publishing, 1992.
Greenway, Theresa. *Amazing Bears*. Knopf Books, 1992.
Helmer, Diana Star. *Black Bears*. Rosen-Powerkids Press, 1997.
Helmer, Diana Star. *Brown Bears*. Rosen-Powerkids Press, 1997.
Helmer, Diana Star. *Polar Bears*. Rosen-Powerkids Press, 1997.
Lynch, Wayne. *Bears, Bears, Bears*. Firefly Books, 1995.
Mathews, Downs and Dan, Guravich. *Polar Bear Cubs*. Simon & Schuster, 1989.
McIntyre, Rick. *Grizzly Cub: Five Years in the Life of a Bear*. Northwest Books, 1990.
Patent, Dorothy H. *Bears of the Wild*. Holiday House, 1980.

Music

Kennedy, Jimmy (book and record). *Teddy Bear's Picnic*. Green Tiger Press, 1983.
Glaser, Tom, editor. *Treasury of Songs for Children*, Doubleday, 1964.
"The Bear Went Over the Mountain." http://geocities.com/soogal99/bearssongs.html

Answer Key

Page 9
Where is My Teddy?

Page 10
Words that Rhyme
bear—pear
rake—cake
can—fan

Page 17
Four Season Fun
(Answers may vary.)
Spring—Bears come out of their dens or caves.
Summer—Mother bears teach their cubs to find food and be safe.
Fall—Bears eat a lot to get fat.
Winter—Bears sleep in their dens or caves.

Page 18
Which Bear?
black bear:
I am a good tree climber.
I like to eat honey, ants, flowers and nuts.
brown bear:
I am sometimes called a grizzly bear.
I have very long claws to catch fish.
polar bear:
I am a big white bear.
I hunt walrus and seals.

Page 27
Polar Bear Maze

Page 36
It Starts With a **B** . . .
B words: Bear, Bunny, Bee, Bird

Page 37
Bear Counters
1. 4
2. 2
3. 3
4. 5

Page 40
Before and After

Before:	After:	Between:
2,3	5,6	4,5,6
8,9	1,2	1,2,3
1,2	7,8	3,4,5
4,5	3,4	
6,7	4,5	
3,4	8,9	
9,10	9,10	
7,8	6,7	
6,7	2,3	
5,6	10,11	

Page 45
Bear Habitat
(Answers will vary depending on bear selected.)
Live—cave, iceberg
Eat—honey, ants, flowers, nuts, mice, walrus, seals, fish
Sleep—cave, ice cave, iceberg

Page 45
How Big is a Bear?
(Answers will vary.)
Smaller Than a Bear
children, foods, toys
Bigger Than a Bear
House, School, Store, Mountain

Page 47
What do Bears Eat?
ants, mice, seals, honey, berries, fish

Page 52
Us and the Bear
(Answers will vary.)